50 Dairy Free and Delicious Recipes

By: Kelly Johnson

Table of Contents

- Chickpea and Spinach Curry
- Grilled Chicken with Mango Salsa
- Vegan Tacos with Black Beans and Guacamole
- Sweet Potato and Lentil Soup
- Spaghetti Squash with Tomato Basil Sauce
- Cauliflower Fried Rice
- Lentil and Vegetable Stew
- Zucchini Noodles with Avocado Pesto
- Baked Lemon Herb Salmon
- Vegan Pad Thai
- Stuffed Bell Peppers with Quinoa and Veggies
- Coconut Curry Chicken
- Vegan Buddha Bowl
- Spicy Cauliflower Tacos
- Mango Chicken Salad
- Vegan Lentil Bolognese
- Sweet Potato and Black Bean Chili
- Grilled Shrimp with Cilantro Lime Rice
- Vegan Stuffed Mushrooms
- Almond-Crusted Chicken with Roasted Veggies
- Vegetable Stir-Fry with Tofu
- Spicy Chickpea and Avocado Salad
- Crispy Baked Eggplant Fries
- Vegan Mushroom Stroganoff
- Grilled Portobello Mushroom Burgers
- Vegan Taco Salad
- Butternut Squash Soup
- Zucchini and Chickpea Fritters
- Chicken and Broccoli Stir-Fry
- Vegan Jackfruit Tacos
- Thai-Inspired Chicken Salad
- Roasted Vegetable and Quinoa Bowl
- Coconut-Lime Chicken
- Vegan Chickpea Salad Sandwich
- Vegan Cauliflower Tacos with Avocado

- Baked Sweet Potatoes with Avocado and Salsa
- Curry Spiced Roasted Cauliflower
- Spaghetti Squash Primavera
- Miso-Glazed Salmon with Rice Noodles
- Shredded Beef and Avocado Lettuce Wraps
- Vegan Avocado Toast with Tomato
- Crispy Chickpea Salad
- Thai Basil Chicken
- Coconut Milk and Chickpea Soup
- Grilled Tofu Skewers
- Cabbage Stir-Fry with Peanut Sauce
- Spaghetti with Roasted Garlic and Spinach
- Vegan Sweet Potato Shepherd's Pie
- BBQ Grilled Chicken with Roasted Sweet Potatoes
- Mango and Black Bean Salad

Chickpea and Spinach Curry

Ingredients:

- 1 can (15 oz) chickpeas, drained and rinsed
- 3 cups fresh spinach
- 1 tablespoon olive oil
- 1 onion, diced
- 2 cloves garlic, minced
- 1 tablespoon ginger, grated
- 1 can (14 oz) diced tomatoes
- 1 teaspoon ground cumin
- 1 teaspoon ground turmeric
- 1 teaspoon garam masala
- 1/2 teaspoon chili powder (optional)
- Salt and pepper, to taste
- 1/2 cup coconut milk
- Fresh cilantro, chopped (for garnish)

Instructions:

1. **Cook the Aromatics**:
   In a large pan, heat olive oil over medium heat. Add the diced onion, garlic, and ginger. Sauté for 3-4 minutes until fragrant and softened.
2. **Add Spices and Tomatoes**:
   Add the cumin, turmeric, garam masala, and chili powder (if using). Stir for 1 minute, then add the diced tomatoes. Simmer for 5 minutes, letting the flavors meld together.
3. **Add Chickpeas and Spinach**:
   Stir in the chickpeas and spinach. Cook for another 5-7 minutes until the spinach is wilted and the chickpeas are heated through.
4. **Add Coconut Milk**:
   Pour in the coconut milk and stir to combine. Simmer for another 5 minutes, then season with salt and pepper to taste.
5. **Serve**:
   Garnish with fresh cilantro and serve with rice or naan.

Grilled Chicken with Mango Salsa

Ingredients:

- 2 boneless, skinless chicken breasts
- 1 tablespoon olive oil
- Salt and pepper, to taste
- 1 ripe mango, peeled and diced
- 1/4 cup red onion, diced
- 1 small red bell pepper, diced
- 1/4 cup cilantro, chopped
- 1 tablespoon lime juice
- 1/2 teaspoon chili powder (optional)

Instructions:

1. **Grill the Chicken**:
   Preheat your grill to medium-high heat. Rub the chicken breasts with olive oil, salt, and pepper. Grill the chicken for 6-7 minutes per side until fully cooked and the internal temperature reaches 165°F (75°C).
2. **Make the Mango Salsa**:
   In a bowl, combine the diced mango, red onion, red bell pepper, cilantro, lime juice, and chili powder (if using). Stir well to combine.
3. **Serve**:
   Top the grilled chicken with the mango salsa and serve with your favorite side.

Vegan Tacos with Black Beans and Guacamole

Ingredients:

- 1 can (15 oz) black beans, drained and rinsed
- 1 tablespoon olive oil
- 1 teaspoon ground cumin
- 1 teaspoon chili powder
- Salt and pepper, to taste
- 8 small corn tortillas
- 1 avocado, mashed
- 1 tablespoon lime juice
- 1/4 cup cilantro, chopped
- Salsa (optional)

Instructions:

1. **Prepare the Black Beans**:
   Heat olive oil in a skillet over medium heat. Add the black beans, cumin, chili powder, salt, and pepper. Cook for 5-7 minutes, stirring occasionally, until heated through.
2. **Prepare the Guacamole**:
   In a bowl, mash the avocado with lime juice and cilantro. Season with salt to taste.
3. **Assemble the Tacos**:
   Warm the tortillas in a skillet or microwave. Fill each tortilla with a spoonful of black beans and top with guacamole. Add salsa if desired.
4. **Serve**:
   Serve the tacos with additional cilantro or lime wedges.

Sweet Potato and Lentil Soup

Ingredients:

- 2 medium sweet potatoes, peeled and diced
- 1 cup dry lentils, rinsed
- 1 onion, diced
- 2 carrots, diced
- 2 celery stalks, diced
- 2 cloves garlic, minced
- 1 teaspoon ground cumin
- 1 teaspoon turmeric
- 4 cups vegetable broth
- Salt and pepper, to taste
- Fresh parsley, chopped (for garnish)

Instructions:

1. **Sauté the Vegetables**:
   In a large pot, heat olive oil over medium heat. Add the onion, carrots, and celery. Sauté for 5-7 minutes until softened. Add the garlic and cook for another 1 minute.
2. **Add the Spices and Broth**:
   Add the cumin and turmeric to the pot and stir to coat the vegetables. Pour in the vegetable broth and bring to a boil.
3. **Cook the Soup**:
   Add the diced sweet potatoes and lentils to the pot. Reduce the heat and simmer for 25-30 minutes, until the sweet potatoes are tender and the lentils are fully cooked.
4. **Blend (optional)**:
   For a creamier texture, use an immersion blender to partially blend the soup, leaving some chunks. Alternatively, blend a portion of the soup in a blender and return it to the pot.
5. **Serve**:
   Season with salt and pepper to taste. Garnish with fresh parsley and serve hot.

Spaghetti Squash with Tomato Basil Sauce

Ingredients:

- 1 medium spaghetti squash
- 2 tablespoons olive oil
- Salt and pepper, to taste
- 1 can (14 oz) crushed tomatoes
- 1/4 cup fresh basil, chopped
- 2 cloves garlic, minced
- 1/4 teaspoon red pepper flakes (optional)

Instructions:

1. **Prepare the Spaghetti Squash:**
   Preheat your oven to 400°F (200°C). Cut the spaghetti squash in half lengthwise and remove the seeds. Drizzle with olive oil, salt, and pepper. Place the squash halves cut-side down on a baking sheet and roast for 35-40 minutes, or until tender.
2. **Make the Tomato Sauce:**
   In a saucepan, heat olive oil over medium heat. Add the garlic and sauté for 1 minute. Add the crushed tomatoes, basil, and red pepper flakes (if using). Simmer for 10 minutes, stirring occasionally.
3. **Assemble the Dish:**
   Once the spaghetti squash is cooked, use a fork to scrape the flesh into spaghetti-like strands. Top with the tomato basil sauce and serve.

Cauliflower Fried Rice

Ingredients:

- 1 medium cauliflower, grated into rice-sized pieces (or use pre-riced cauliflower)
- 2 tablespoons sesame oil
- 2 cloves garlic, minced
- 1/2 cup peas and carrots (frozen or fresh)
- 2 eggs, scrambled
- 2 tablespoons soy sauce (or coconut aminos)
- 2 green onions, chopped

Instructions:

1. **Cook the Cauliflower Rice**:
   In a large skillet, heat sesame oil over medium heat. Add the garlic and sauté for 1 minute. Add the cauliflower rice and cook for 5-7 minutes until softened.
2. **Add the Vegetables and Eggs**:
   Push the cauliflower rice to one side of the pan and scramble the eggs on the other side. Add the peas and carrots and cook for 3-4 minutes until tender.
3. **Season and Serve**:
   Add the soy sauce and green onions to the pan. Stir everything together and cook for another 2-3 minutes. Serve hot.

Lentil and Vegetable Stew

Ingredients:

- 1 cup dry lentils, rinsed
- 2 cups chopped vegetables (carrots, celery, zucchini, etc.)
- 1 onion, diced
- 2 cloves garlic, minced
- 1 can (14 oz) diced tomatoes
- 4 cups vegetable broth
- 1 teaspoon dried thyme
- 1 teaspoon ground cumin
- Salt and pepper, to taste

Instructions:

1. **Sauté the Vegetables**:
   In a large pot, heat olive oil over medium heat. Add the onion, garlic, and chopped vegetables. Sauté for 5-7 minutes until softened.
2. **Add the Lentils and Spices**:
   Add the lentils, diced tomatoes, vegetable broth, thyme, cumin, salt, and pepper to the pot. Stir well and bring to a boil.
3. **Simmer the Stew**:
   Reduce the heat and let the stew simmer for 25-30 minutes, or until the lentils and vegetables are tender.
4. **Serve**:
   Season with additional salt and pepper to taste and serve hot.

Zucchini Noodles with Avocado Pesto

Ingredients:

- 4 medium zucchinis, spiralized into noodles
- 1 ripe avocado
- 1/2 cup fresh basil leaves
- 2 tablespoons lemon juice
- 2 cloves garlic
- 1/4 cup olive oil
- Salt and pepper, to taste
- Pine nuts (optional, for garnish)

Instructions:

1. **Prepare the Pesto**:
   In a food processor, blend the avocado, basil, lemon juice, garlic, olive oil, salt, and pepper until smooth and creamy.
2. **Cook the Zucchini Noodles**:
   Heat a little olive oil in a large skillet over medium heat. Add the zucchini noodles and sauté for 2-3 minutes until tender but still firm.
3. **Toss and Serve**:
   Toss the zucchini noodles with the avocado pesto. Garnish with pine nuts, if desired, and serve immediately.

Baked Lemon Herb Salmon

Ingredients:

- 4 salmon fillets
- 1 tablespoon olive oil
- Juice and zest of 1 lemon
- 2 cloves garlic, minced
- 1 teaspoon dried thyme
- Salt and pepper, to taste

Instructions:

1. **Prepare the Salmon**:
   Preheat the oven to 400°F (200°C). Place the salmon fillets on a baking sheet lined with parchment paper.
2. **Season the Fish**:
   Drizzle the olive oil over the salmon and sprinkle with lemon juice, zest, garlic, thyme, salt, and pepper.
3. **Bake the Salmon**:
   Bake for 12-15 minutes, or until the salmon flakes easily with a fork.
4. **Serve**:
   Serve with your favorite vegetables or a side salad.

Vegan Pad Thai

Ingredients:

- 8 oz rice noodles
- 1 tablespoon olive oil
- 1 cup shredded carrots
- 1 red bell pepper, sliced
- 2 cloves garlic, minced
- 1 tablespoon soy sauce
- 1 tablespoon peanut butter
- 1 tablespoon lime juice
- 1 teaspoon maple syrup
- Crushed peanuts, cilantro, and lime wedges (for garnish)

Instructions:

1. **Prepare the Noodles**:
   Cook the rice noodles according to the package instructions, then set aside.
2. **Cook the Vegetables**:
   Heat olive oil in a large skillet over medium heat. Add the shredded carrots and red bell pepper. Sauté for 5 minutes until softened.
3. **Make the Sauce**:
   In a small bowl, whisk together the soy sauce, peanut butter, lime juice, and maple syrup.
4. **Combine**:
   Add the cooked noodles and sauce to the skillet. Toss to combine and heat through.
5. **Serve**:
   Garnish with crushed peanuts, cilantro, and lime wedges. Serve hot.

Stuffed Bell Peppers with Quinoa and Veggies

Ingredients:

- 4 bell peppers, tops cut off and seeds removed
- 1 cup quinoa, cooked
- 1 can (15 oz) black beans, drained and rinsed
- 1 cup corn kernels (fresh or frozen)
- 1 cup diced tomatoes
- 1 onion, diced
- 1 tablespoon olive oil
- 1 teaspoon cumin
- 1 teaspoon paprika
- Salt and pepper, to taste
- 1/4 cup fresh cilantro, chopped
- 1/2 cup shredded cheese (optional)

Instructions:

1. **Prepare the Bell Peppers**:
   Preheat the oven to 375°F (190°C). Place the bell peppers in a baking dish.
2. **Make the Filling**:
   In a skillet, heat olive oil over medium heat. Add the diced onion and cook until softened, about 5 minutes. Stir in the cooked quinoa, black beans, corn, diced tomatoes, cumin, paprika, salt, and pepper. Cook for another 5 minutes, stirring occasionally.
3. **Stuff the Peppers**:
   Spoon the quinoa and veggie mixture into each bell pepper, packing it tightly. Top with shredded cheese, if using.
4. **Bake the Peppers**:
   Cover the baking dish with foil and bake for 25-30 minutes, until the peppers are tender.
5. **Serve**:
   Garnish with fresh cilantro and serve.

Coconut Curry Chicken

Ingredients:

- 4 boneless, skinless chicken breasts, cut into chunks
- 1 tablespoon olive oil
- 1 onion, diced
- 2 cloves garlic, minced
- 1 tablespoon ginger, grated
- 1 can (14 oz) coconut milk
- 1 tablespoon red curry paste
- 1 tablespoon soy sauce
- 1 teaspoon turmeric
- Salt and pepper, to taste
- Fresh cilantro, chopped (for garnish)
- 1 tablespoon lime juice

Instructions:

1. **Cook the Chicken:**
   In a large skillet, heat olive oil over medium heat. Add the chicken pieces and cook until browned and cooked through, about 7-8 minutes. Remove and set aside.
2. **Make the Sauce:**
   In the same skillet, add onion, garlic, and ginger. Sauté for 3-4 minutes until softened. Stir in the curry paste, soy sauce, turmeric, coconut milk, salt, and pepper. Simmer for 5 minutes.
3. **Combine:**
   Add the cooked chicken back into the skillet and stir to coat in the sauce. Simmer for another 5 minutes.
4. **Serve:**
   Finish with a squeeze of lime juice and garnish with fresh cilantro. Serve with rice or vegetables.

Vegan Buddha Bowl

Ingredients:

- 1 cup cooked quinoa or rice
- 1 cup roasted sweet potatoes, cubed
- 1/2 cup chickpeas, roasted
- 1 avocado, sliced
- 1 cup spinach or mixed greens
- 1/2 cup shredded carrots
- 1 tablespoon tahini
- 1 tablespoon lemon juice
- Salt and pepper, to taste

Instructions:

1. **Prepare the Ingredients**:
   Roast the sweet potatoes and chickpeas at 400°F (200°C) for 25 minutes, drizzling with olive oil, salt, and pepper.
2. **Assemble the Bowl**:
   In a large bowl, layer quinoa or rice, roasted sweet potatoes, roasted chickpeas, avocado slices, spinach, and shredded carrots.
3. **Make the Dressing**:
   Whisk together tahini, lemon juice, salt, and pepper. Add a little water if needed to thin it out.
4. **Serve**:
   Drizzle the dressing over the bowl and serve immediately.

Spicy Cauliflower Tacos

Ingredients:

- 1 medium cauliflower, cut into florets
- 1 tablespoon olive oil
- 1 teaspoon chili powder
- 1 teaspoon smoked paprika
- 1/2 teaspoon cumin
- Salt and pepper, to taste
- 8 small corn tortillas
- 1/4 cup red cabbage, shredded
- 1/4 cup fresh cilantro, chopped
- 1 avocado, sliced
- Lime wedges

Instructions:

1. **Prepare the Cauliflower**:
   Preheat the oven to 400°F (200°C). Toss cauliflower florets with olive oil, chili powder, paprika, cumin, salt, and pepper. Spread on a baking sheet and roast for 25-30 minutes, until crispy and golden.
2. **Assemble the Tacos**:
   Warm the tortillas and fill each with roasted cauliflower, shredded cabbage, avocado, and fresh cilantro.
3. **Serve**:
   Squeeze lime wedges over the tacos and serve immediately.

Mango Chicken Salad

Ingredients:

- 2 boneless, skinless chicken breasts, grilled and sliced
- 1 mango, peeled and diced
- 4 cups mixed greens
- 1/2 red onion, thinly sliced
- 1/4 cup cucumber, sliced
- 1 tablespoon olive oil
- 1 tablespoon balsamic vinegar
- 1 teaspoon honey
- Salt and pepper, to taste

Instructions:

1. **Grill the Chicken**:
   Season the chicken breasts with salt and pepper and grill until fully cooked, about 6-7 minutes per side. Slice thinly.
2. **Prepare the Salad**:
   In a large bowl, combine mixed greens, mango, red onion, cucumber, and grilled chicken.
3. **Make the Dressing**:
   In a small bowl, whisk together olive oil, balsamic vinegar, honey, salt, and pepper.
4. **Serve**:
   Toss the salad with the dressing and serve immediately.

Vegan Lentil Bolognese

Ingredients:

- 1 cup dry lentils, rinsed
- 1 onion, diced
- 2 cloves garlic, minced
- 1 carrot, diced
- 1 celery stalk, diced
- 1 can (14 oz) crushed tomatoes
- 1 tablespoon tomato paste
- 1 teaspoon dried oregano
- 1 teaspoon dried basil
- Salt and pepper, to taste
- Olive oil for cooking
- Cooked pasta (spaghetti or any preferred kind)

Instructions:

1. **Cook the Lentils:**
   In a pot, add lentils and cover with water. Bring to a boil and then reduce heat. Simmer for 20-25 minutes until lentils are tender, then drain.
2. **Sauté the Vegetables:**
   In a large skillet, heat olive oil over medium heat. Add onion, garlic, carrot, and celery. Cook for 5-7 minutes until softened.
3. **Make the Sauce:**
   Stir in crushed tomatoes, tomato paste, oregano, basil, salt, and pepper. Simmer for 15 minutes. Add the cooked lentils and simmer for another 5 minutes.
4. **Serve:**
   Serve the bolognese sauce over cooked pasta.

Sweet Potato and Black Bean Chili

Ingredients:

- 2 medium sweet potatoes, peeled and cubed
- 1 can (15 oz) black beans, drained and rinsed
- 1 can (14 oz) diced tomatoes
- 1 onion, diced
- 2 cloves garlic, minced
- 1 tablespoon olive oil
- 1 teaspoon ground cumin
- 1 teaspoon chili powder
- 1/2 teaspoon smoked paprika
- Salt and pepper, to taste
- 4 cups vegetable broth
- Fresh cilantro, chopped (for garnish)

Instructions:

1. **Cook the Vegetables**:
   In a large pot, heat olive oil over medium heat. Add onion and garlic, sauté for 3 minutes. Add sweet potatoes, cumin, chili powder, paprika, salt, and pepper, and stir to combine.
2. **Simmer the Chili**:
   Add diced tomatoes, black beans, vegetable broth, and bring to a boil. Reduce heat and simmer for 25-30 minutes, until sweet potatoes are tender.
3. **Serve**:
   Garnish with fresh cilantro and serve hot.

Grilled Shrimp with Cilantro Lime Rice

Ingredients:

- 1 lb shrimp, peeled and deveined
- 1 tablespoon olive oil
- 1 teaspoon chili powder
- Salt and pepper, to taste
- 2 cups cooked rice (preferably jasmine or basmati)
- 1 tablespoon fresh lime juice
- 1/4 cup fresh cilantro, chopped

Instructions:

1. **Grill the Shrimp**:
   Preheat the grill to medium-high heat. Toss shrimp with olive oil, chili powder, salt, and pepper. Grill for 2-3 minutes per side until pink and cooked through.
2. **Make the Cilantro Lime Rice**:
   Fluff the cooked rice with a fork and stir in lime juice and cilantro.
3. **Serve**:
   Serve the grilled shrimp on top of the cilantro lime rice.

Vegan Stuffed Mushrooms

Ingredients:

- 12 large mushrooms, stems removed
- 1 cup cooked quinoa or rice
- 1/2 cup spinach, chopped
- 1/4 cup nutritional yeast
- 1 tablespoon olive oil
- 1 clove garlic, minced
- Salt and pepper, to taste

Instructions:

1. **Prepare the Filling:**
   In a skillet, heat olive oil over medium heat. Add garlic and spinach, sauté until spinach wilts. Stir in quinoa or rice, nutritional yeast, salt, and pepper.
2. **Stuff the Mushrooms:**
   Spoon the filling into each mushroom cap.
3. **Bake the Mushrooms:**
   Preheat the oven to 375°F (190°C). Arrange the stuffed mushrooms on a baking sheet and bake for 15-20 minutes until tender.
4. **Serve:**
   Serve as an appetizer or main dish.

Almond-Crusted Chicken with Roasted Veggies

Ingredients:

- 4 boneless, skinless chicken breasts
- 1 cup almond meal
- 1 egg, beaten
- 1 tablespoon olive oil
- Salt and pepper, to taste
- 2 cups mixed vegetables (e.g., carrots, zucchini, bell peppers), chopped

Instructions:

1. **Prepare the Chicken**:
   Preheat the oven to 400°F (200°C). Dip each chicken breast into the beaten egg, then coat with almond meal.
2. **Roast the Veggies**:
   Toss the chopped vegetables with olive oil, salt, and pepper. Spread on a baking sheet.
3. **Bake**:
   Place the almond-crusted chicken on the same baking sheet and bake for 25-30 minutes, until the chicken is cooked through and vegetables are tender.
4. **Serve**:
   Serve the almond-crusted chicken with roasted veggies.

Vegetable Stir-Fry with Tofu

Ingredients:

- 1 block firm tofu, pressed and cubed
- 1 tablespoon olive oil
- 1 onion, sliced
- 1 bell pepper, sliced
- 1 zucchini, sliced
- 1 cup broccoli florets
- 1/2 cup snap peas
- 2 cloves garlic, minced
- 2 tablespoons soy sauce
- 1 tablespoon sesame oil
- 1 tablespoon rice vinegar
- 1 teaspoon honey or maple syrup (optional)
- 1 teaspoon fresh ginger, grated
- Sesame seeds, for garnish

Instructions:

1. **Prepare the Tofu**:
   Press the tofu to remove excess moisture, then cut it into cubes. Heat olive oil in a large skillet over medium heat. Add the tofu and cook until golden and crispy on all sides, about 8-10 minutes. Remove from the pan and set aside.
2. **Sauté the Vegetables**:
   In the same skillet, add more oil if needed, then sauté the onion, bell pepper, zucchini, broccoli, and snap peas for 5-6 minutes until they are tender but still crisp.
3. **Make the Sauce**:
   Add the garlic and ginger, cooking for 1 minute until fragrant. Stir in soy sauce, sesame oil, rice vinegar, and honey/maple syrup.
4. **Combine**:
   Add the tofu back to the pan and toss everything to coat in the sauce. Cook for another 2-3 minutes.
5. **Serve**:
   Garnish with sesame seeds and serve hot with rice or noodles.

Spicy Chickpea and Avocado Salad

Ingredients:

- 1 can (15 oz) chickpeas, drained and rinsed
- 1 tablespoon olive oil
- 1 teaspoon smoked paprika
- 1/2 teaspoon chili powder
- 1/4 teaspoon cayenne pepper (optional)
- Salt and pepper, to taste
- 1 avocado, diced
- 1 cup cherry tomatoes, halved
- 1/2 cucumber, diced
- 1/4 red onion, thinly sliced
- Fresh cilantro, for garnish
- 1 tablespoon lime juice

Instructions:

1. **Prepare the Chickpeas:**
   Heat olive oil in a pan over medium heat. Add the chickpeas and season with smoked paprika, chili powder, cayenne pepper, salt, and pepper. Cook for 5-6 minutes until crispy and golden.
2. **Make the Salad:**
   In a bowl, combine diced avocado, cherry tomatoes, cucumber, and red onion.
3. **Combine:**
   Add the crispy chickpeas to the salad and toss gently. Drizzle with lime juice and garnish with fresh cilantro.
4. **Serve:**
   Serve the salad immediately or chill in the fridge for a refreshing, spicy meal.

Crispy Baked Eggplant Fries

Ingredients:

- 2 medium eggplants, sliced into fries
- 1/2 cup almond flour
- 1/2 cup panko breadcrumbs (use gluten-free for a gluten-free version)
- 1 teaspoon garlic powder
- 1 teaspoon paprika
- Salt and pepper, to taste
- 1 egg, beaten
- Olive oil spray

Instructions:

1. **Preheat the Oven:**
   Preheat your oven to 400°F (200°C). Line a baking sheet with parchment paper.
2. **Prepare the Coating:**
   In a shallow bowl, combine almond flour, panko breadcrumbs, garlic powder, paprika, salt, and pepper.
3. **Coat the Eggplant:**
   Dip the eggplant slices into the beaten egg, then coat them with the breadcrumb mixture. Place the coated fries onto the baking sheet.
4. **Bake:**
   Lightly spray the fries with olive oil. Bake for 25-30 minutes, flipping halfway through, until golden and crispy.
5. **Serve:**
   Serve with a dipping sauce such as marinara or ranch.

Vegan Mushroom Stroganoff

Ingredients:

- 2 tablespoons olive oil
- 1 onion, diced
- 3 cloves garlic, minced
- 8 oz mushrooms, sliced (button, cremini, or a mix)
- 1 teaspoon smoked paprika
- 1 teaspoon dried thyme
- 1/2 cup vegetable broth
- 1/2 cup canned coconut milk
- 2 tablespoons nutritional yeast (optional)
- Salt and pepper, to taste
- Fresh parsley, for garnish
- Cooked pasta or rice, to serve

Instructions:

1. **Sauté the Aromatics**:
   Heat olive oil in a large pan over medium heat. Add onion and garlic, and cook until softened, about 3 minutes.
2. **Cook the Mushrooms**:
   Add the sliced mushrooms, smoked paprika, and thyme. Cook for 5-7 minutes until the mushrooms release their moisture and begin to brown.
3. **Make the Sauce**:
   Pour in the vegetable broth and coconut milk, stirring to combine. Simmer for 5-7 minutes until the sauce thickens.
4. **Finish the Dish**:
   Stir in nutritional yeast (if using), season with salt and pepper, and simmer for another 2 minutes.
5. **Serve**:
   Serve the mushroom stroganoff over cooked pasta or rice, garnished with fresh parsley.

Grilled Portobello Mushroom Burgers

Ingredients:

- 4 large portobello mushroom caps, stems removed
- 2 tablespoons olive oil
- 1 tablespoon balsamic vinegar
- 1 teaspoon garlic powder
- Salt and pepper, to taste
- 4 whole-grain buns or lettuce leaves (for low-carb option)
- 1 tomato, sliced
- 1 avocado, sliced
- Fresh spinach or arugula
- Vegan mayo or mustard, for topping

Instructions:

1. **Prepare the Mushrooms:**
   Preheat the grill or grill pan to medium-high heat. In a bowl, combine olive oil, balsamic vinegar, garlic powder, salt, and pepper. Brush the mixture onto both sides of the mushroom caps.
2. **Grill the Mushrooms:**
   Grill the mushrooms for 4-5 minutes per side until tender and slightly charred.
3. **Assemble the Burgers:**
   Place each grilled mushroom cap on a bun or lettuce leaf. Top with tomato slices, avocado, fresh spinach, and a spread of vegan mayo or mustard.
4. **Serve:**
   Serve immediately as a hearty burger alternative.

Vegan Taco Salad

Ingredients:

- 2 cups mixed greens
- 1 can (15 oz) black beans, drained and rinsed
- 1 cup corn kernels (fresh or frozen)
- 1 avocado, diced
- 1/2 red onion, thinly sliced
- 1/2 cup cherry tomatoes, halved
- 1 tablespoon olive oil
- 1 teaspoon ground cumin
- 1 teaspoon chili powder
- Salt and pepper, to taste
- 1/4 cup salsa (for dressing)

Instructions:

1. **Sauté the Black Beans and Corn:**
   In a skillet, heat olive oil over medium heat. Add black beans, corn, cumin, chili powder, salt, and pepper. Sauté for 5-7 minutes until heated through.
2. **Assemble the Salad:**
   In a large bowl, combine mixed greens, diced avocado, red onion, cherry tomatoes, and the sautéed black bean and corn mixture.
3. **Serve:**
   Top with salsa and serve immediately.

Butternut Squash Soup

Ingredients:

- 1 medium butternut squash, peeled and cubed
- 1 tablespoon olive oil
- 1 onion, diced
- 2 cloves garlic, minced
- 4 cups vegetable broth
- 1 teaspoon ground cinnamon
- Salt and pepper, to taste
- 1/2 cup coconut milk or cream (optional for creaminess)

Instructions:

1. **Roast the Squash**:
   Preheat the oven to 400°F (200°C). Toss the butternut squash cubes with olive oil, salt, and pepper. Spread on a baking sheet and roast for 25-30 minutes until tender.
2. **Sauté the Aromatics**:
   In a large pot, sauté onion and garlic in olive oil over medium heat for 5 minutes until softened.
3. **Make the Soup**:
   Add the roasted squash to the pot, then pour in the vegetable broth and cinnamon. Bring to a boil, then reduce heat and simmer for 10 minutes.
4. **Blend the Soup**:
   Using an immersion blender or regular blender, blend the soup until smooth. Stir in coconut milk for extra creaminess, and adjust seasoning as needed.
5. **Serve**:
   Serve hot, optionally garnished with a swirl of coconut milk.

Zucchini and Chickpea Fritters

Ingredients:

- 1 medium zucchini, grated
- 1 can (15 oz) chickpeas, drained and mashed
- 1/4 cup flour (use chickpea flour for a gluten-free version)
- 1 egg (or flax egg for vegan version)
- 1 teaspoon ground cumin
- 1 teaspoon paprika
- Salt and pepper, to taste
- Olive oil, for frying

Instructions:

1. **Prepare the Mixture**:
   In a bowl, combine grated zucchini, mashed chickpeas, flour, egg (or flax egg), cumin, paprika, salt, and pepper. Mix until well combined.
2. **Form the Fritters**:
   Form the mixture into small patties or fritters.
3. **Fry**:
   Heat olive oil in a pan over medium heat. Cook the fritters for 3-4 minutes on each side, until golden brown.
4. **Serve**:
   Serve the fritters with a side of yogurt or avocado dip.

Chicken and Broccoli Stir-Fry

Ingredients:

- 2 chicken breasts, sliced thinly
- 2 tablespoons soy sauce
- 1 tablespoon sesame oil
- 1 tablespoon rice vinegar
- 1 teaspoon garlic powder
- 2 cups broccoli florets
- 1 red bell pepper, sliced
- 1 carrot, julienned
- 1 tablespoon olive oil

Instructions:

1. **Cook the Chicken**:
   In a large skillet or wok, heat olive oil over medium-high heat. Add the chicken slices and cook for 5-7 minutes until golden and cooked through.
2. **Sauté the Vegetables**:
   Add the broccoli, bell pepper, and carrot to the pan. Cook for 3-4 minutes until tender-crisp.
3. **Add the Sauce**:
   Stir in soy sauce, sesame oil, rice vinegar, and garlic powder. Toss everything to coat evenly.
4. **Serve**:
   Serve the stir-fry over rice or enjoy as is for a low-carb option.

Vegan Jackfruit Tacos

Ingredients:

- 2 cans (20 oz each) young green jackfruit, drained and shredded
- 1 tablespoon olive oil
- 1 onion, sliced
- 2 cloves garlic, minced
- 1 teaspoon ground cumin
- 1 teaspoon chili powder
- 1/2 teaspoon smoked paprika
- 1/2 teaspoon ground coriander
- Salt and pepper, to taste
- 1 tablespoon lime juice
- Corn tortillas
- Toppings: shredded cabbage, salsa, avocado, cilantro, lime wedges

Instructions:

1. **Prepare the Jackfruit**:
   Heat olive oil in a large skillet over medium heat. Add the sliced onion and garlic, sautéing until softened (about 3-4 minutes). Add the shredded jackfruit, cumin, chili powder, smoked paprika, ground coriander, salt, and pepper. Stir well and cook for 8-10 minutes, allowing the jackfruit to absorb the spices and soften.
2. **Add Lime**:
   Stir in the lime juice and cook for another 2 minutes.
3. **Assemble the Tacos**:
   Warm the corn tortillas in a skillet or microwave. Spoon the jackfruit mixture onto the tortillas and top with shredded cabbage, salsa, avocado, and cilantro.
4. **Serve**:
   Serve immediately with extra lime wedges on the side.

Thai-Inspired Chicken Salad

Ingredients:

- 2 boneless, skinless chicken breasts, grilled and sliced
- 4 cups mixed greens
- 1 carrot, julienned
- 1 cucumber, thinly sliced
- 1/4 red onion, thinly sliced
- 1/4 cup fresh cilantro, chopped
- 1/4 cup chopped peanuts or cashews
- 1 tablespoon sesame oil
- 2 tablespoons rice vinegar
- 1 tablespoon soy sauce or tamari
- 1 tablespoon honey or maple syrup
- 1 teaspoon grated fresh ginger
- 1 teaspoon lime juice

Instructions:

1. **Prepare the Salad**:
   In a large bowl, toss together the mixed greens, carrot, cucumber, red onion, and cilantro.
2. **Make the Dressing**:
   In a small bowl, whisk together sesame oil, rice vinegar, soy sauce, honey (or maple syrup), ginger, and lime juice until well combined.
3. **Assemble the Salad**:
   Top the salad with the grilled chicken slices, chopped peanuts or cashews, and drizzle with the dressing.
4. **Serve**:
   Serve immediately for a light, refreshing meal.

Roasted Vegetable and Quinoa Bowl

Ingredients:

- 1 cup quinoa, rinsed
- 2 cups water or vegetable broth
- 1 zucchini, diced
- 1 bell pepper, diced
- 1 cup cherry tomatoes, halved
- 1 red onion, sliced
- 1 tablespoon olive oil
- 1 teaspoon dried oregano
- Salt and pepper, to taste
- 1/4 cup feta cheese (optional for non-vegan)
- Fresh parsley, for garnish

Instructions:

1. **Cook the Quinoa**:
   In a saucepan, bring water or vegetable broth to a boil. Add the quinoa, cover, and reduce heat. Simmer for 15 minutes, or until the quinoa is cooked and the liquid is absorbed. Fluff with a fork and set aside.
2. **Roast the Vegetables**:
   Preheat the oven to 400°F (200°C). Toss the zucchini, bell pepper, cherry tomatoes, and red onion with olive oil, oregano, salt, and pepper. Spread them out on a baking sheet and roast for 20-25 minutes, stirring halfway through.
3. **Assemble the Bowl**:
   Divide the quinoa between bowls and top with the roasted vegetables. Sprinkle with feta cheese (if using) and garnish with fresh parsley.
4. **Serve**:
   Serve warm as a nourishing, filling bowl.

Coconut-Lime Chicken

Ingredients:

- 4 boneless, skinless chicken breasts
- 1 tablespoon coconut oil
- 1/2 cup coconut milk
- 1 tablespoon lime juice
- 1 teaspoon lime zest
- 1 tablespoon honey or maple syrup
- Salt and pepper, to taste
- Fresh cilantro, for garnish

Instructions:

1. **Cook the Chicken**:
   Heat coconut oil in a skillet over medium heat. Season the chicken breasts with salt and pepper, and cook for 6-7 minutes on each side, until fully cooked and golden brown.
2. **Make the Sauce**:
   In a small bowl, whisk together coconut milk, lime juice, lime zest, and honey. Pour the sauce over the chicken breasts and simmer for 2-3 minutes until heated through.
3. **Serve**:
   Garnish with fresh cilantro and serve the chicken with rice or vegetables.

Vegan Chickpea Salad Sandwich

Ingredients:

- 1 can (15 oz) chickpeas, drained and mashed
- 2 tablespoons vegan mayo
- 1 tablespoon Dijon mustard
- 1 tablespoon lemon juice
- 1/4 red onion, finely diced
- 1/4 cup celery, finely diced
- Salt and pepper, to taste
- 4 slices whole-grain bread
- Lettuce, for garnish

Instructions:

1. **Prepare the Chickpea Salad**:
   In a bowl, mash the chickpeas with a fork until mostly mashed but with some chunks remaining. Add vegan mayo, Dijon mustard, lemon juice, red onion, celery, salt, and pepper. Mix until combined.
2. **Assemble the Sandwiches**:
   Spread the chickpea mixture onto two slices of whole-grain bread. Top with lettuce and another slice of bread.
3. **Serve**:
   Serve immediately or wrap for a lunch on the go.

Vegan Cauliflower Tacos with Avocado

Ingredients:

- 1 small head cauliflower, cut into florets
- 2 tablespoons olive oil
- 1 teaspoon cumin
- 1 teaspoon paprika
- 1/2 teaspoon chili powder
- Salt and pepper, to taste
- 8 corn tortillas
- 1 avocado, sliced
- 1/2 cup red cabbage, shredded
- Fresh cilantro, for garnish
- Lime wedges, for serving

Instructions:

1. **Roast the Cauliflower**:
   Preheat the oven to 400°F (200°C). Toss the cauliflower florets with olive oil, cumin, paprika, chili powder, salt, and pepper. Spread them on a baking sheet and roast for 20-25 minutes, until tender and lightly browned.
2. **Assemble the Tacos**:
   Warm the corn tortillas in a skillet or microwave. Fill each tortilla with roasted cauliflower, sliced avocado, shredded red cabbage, and fresh cilantro.
3. **Serve**:
   Serve with lime wedges for a zesty finish.

Baked Sweet Potatoes with Avocado and Salsa

Ingredients:

- 2 medium sweet potatoes
- 1 avocado, diced
- 1/2 cup salsa
- 1 tablespoon fresh cilantro, chopped
- Salt and pepper, to taste

Instructions:

1. **Bake the Sweet Potatoes**:
   Preheat the oven to 400°F (200°C). Pierce the sweet potatoes with a fork and place them on a baking sheet. Bake for 40-45 minutes until tender.
2. **Prepare the Toppings**:
   While the sweet potatoes bake, dice the avocado and chop the cilantro.
3. **Assemble the Dish**:
   Once the sweet potatoes are done, cut them open and fluff the insides with a fork. Top with diced avocado, salsa, cilantro, and a pinch of salt and pepper.
4. **Serve**:
   Serve warm as a satisfying and nutritious meal.

Curry Spiced Roasted Cauliflower

Ingredients:

- 1 medium cauliflower, cut into florets
- 2 tablespoons olive oil
- 1 teaspoon curry powder
- 1/2 teaspoon cumin
- 1/2 teaspoon turmeric
- Salt and pepper, to taste

Instructions:

1. **Prepare the Cauliflower**:
   Preheat the oven to 400°F (200°C). Toss the cauliflower florets with olive oil, curry powder, cumin, turmeric, salt, and pepper.
2. **Roast the Cauliflower**:
   Spread the cauliflower on a baking sheet and roast for 20-25 minutes, stirring halfway through, until tender and golden.
3. **Serve**:
   Serve as a side dish or over rice for a light meal.

Spaghetti Squash Primavera

Ingredients:

- 1 medium spaghetti squash
- 1 tablespoon olive oil
- 1 zucchini, sliced
- 1 bell pepper, sliced
- 1/2 cup cherry tomatoes, halved
- 1/4 cup fresh basil, chopped
- 1 tablespoon balsamic vinegar
- Salt and pepper, to taste

Instructions:

1. **Prepare the Spaghetti Squash:**
   Preheat the oven to 400°F (200°C). Cut the spaghetti squash in half lengthwise and remove the seeds. Drizzle with olive oil and season with salt and pepper. Place the squash cut-side down on a baking sheet and roast for 30-40 minutes, until tender. Once done, use a fork to scrape the squash into spaghetti-like strands.
2. **Sauté the Vegetables:**
   In a skillet, heat olive oil over medium heat. Add zucchini, bell pepper, and cherry tomatoes. Sauté for 5-7 minutes until the vegetables are tender.
3. **Combine:**
   Toss the roasted spaghetti squash with the sautéed vegetables. Drizzle with balsamic vinegar and top with fresh basil.
4. **Serve:**
   Serve warm as a delicious and light pasta alternative.

Miso-Glazed Salmon with Rice Noodles

Ingredients:

- 4 salmon fillets
- 2 tablespoons white miso paste
- 1 tablespoon soy sauce or tamari
- 1 tablespoon honey or maple syrup
- 1 teaspoon rice vinegar
- 1 tablespoon sesame oil
- 1 tablespoon grated ginger
- 1 teaspoon garlic, minced
- 8 oz rice noodles
- 1/2 cup thinly sliced scallions
- 1 tablespoon sesame seeds (optional)
- Lime wedges, for serving

Instructions:

1. **Prepare the Miso Glaze**:
   In a small bowl, whisk together miso paste, soy sauce, honey, rice vinegar, sesame oil, grated ginger, and garlic until smooth.
2. **Glaze the Salmon**:
   Preheat your oven to 375°F (190°C). Place the salmon fillets on a baking sheet lined with parchment paper. Brush each fillet generously with the miso glaze and bake for 12-15 minutes or until the salmon is cooked through and flakes easily with a fork.
3. **Cook the Rice Noodles**:
   While the salmon is baking, cook the rice noodles according to the package instructions. Drain and set aside.
4. **Assemble the Dish**:
   Serve the salmon over the cooked rice noodles. Garnish with sliced scallions, sesame seeds, and lime wedges.
5. **Serve**:
   Enjoy this flavorful and healthy dish!

Shredded Beef and Avocado Lettuce Wraps

Ingredients:

- 1 lb beef chuck roast
- 1 tablespoon olive oil
- 1 onion, chopped
- 2 cloves garlic, minced
- 1 teaspoon ground cumin
- 1 teaspoon chili powder
- 1/2 teaspoon smoked paprika
- Salt and pepper, to taste
- 1 cup beef broth
- 1 tablespoon lime juice
- 1 avocado, sliced
- Large lettuce leaves (e.g., butter or romaine lettuce)
- Fresh cilantro, for garnish

Instructions:

1. **Cook the Beef**:
   In a large pot or slow cooker, heat olive oil over medium-high heat. Season the beef chuck roast with salt, pepper, cumin, chili powder, and smoked paprika. Sear the beef on all sides until browned, about 5-7 minutes. Add the chopped onion, garlic, and beef broth. Cover and cook on low for 6-8 hours (or 3-4 hours on high in a slow cooker), until the beef is tender and shreds easily.
2. **Shred the Beef**:
   Once the beef is done, remove it from the pot and shred it using two forks.
3. **Assemble the Lettuce Wraps**:
   Place spoonfuls of shredded beef onto large lettuce leaves. Top with avocado slices and fresh cilantro.
4. **Serve**:
   Serve immediately as a light and flavorful meal.

Vegan Avocado Toast with Tomato

Ingredients:

- 2 slices whole grain bread
- 1 ripe avocado
- 1 small tomato, sliced
- Salt and pepper, to taste
- 1 tablespoon olive oil (optional)
- Red pepper flakes, for garnish (optional)

Instructions:

1. **Toast the Bread**:
   Toast the bread slices to your desired level of crispness.
2. **Prepare the Avocado**:
   While the bread is toasting, slice the avocado in half and remove the pit. Scoop the flesh into a bowl and mash with a fork. Season with salt and pepper.
3. **Assemble the Toast**:
   Spread the mashed avocado evenly onto each piece of toasted bread. Top with tomato slices.
4. **Serve**:
   Drizzle with olive oil (optional) and garnish with red pepper flakes if desired. Serve immediately for a quick and healthy meal.

Crispy Chickpea Salad

Ingredients:

- 1 can (15 oz) chickpeas, drained and rinsed
- 2 tablespoons olive oil
- 1 teaspoon smoked paprika
- 1 teaspoon garlic powder
- Salt and pepper, to taste
- 4 cups mixed greens (spinach, arugula, etc.)
- 1 cucumber, diced
- 1/2 cup cherry tomatoes, halved
- 1/4 red onion, thinly sliced
- 1 tablespoon tahini
- 1 tablespoon lemon juice
- 1 teaspoon maple syrup (optional)

Instructions:

1. **Crisp the Chickpeas**:
   Preheat the oven to 400°F (200°C). Pat the chickpeas dry with a paper towel. Toss them with olive oil, smoked paprika, garlic powder, salt, and pepper. Spread them out on a baking sheet in a single layer and bake for 20-25 minutes, shaking the pan halfway through, until crispy.
2. **Prepare the Salad**:
   While the chickpeas are baking, combine mixed greens, cucumber, cherry tomatoes, and red onion in a large bowl.
3. **Make the Dressing**:
   In a small bowl, whisk together tahini, lemon juice, and maple syrup (if using). Add water as needed to reach a pourable consistency. Season with salt and pepper to taste.
4. **Assemble the Salad**:
   Once the chickpeas are crispy, toss them with the salad and drizzle with the tahini dressing.
5. **Serve**:
   Serve immediately for a crunchy, nutritious meal.

Thai Basil Chicken

Ingredients:

- 2 chicken breasts, thinly sliced
- 2 tablespoons vegetable oil
- 3 cloves garlic, minced
- 2-3 Thai bird's eye chilies (or red chili, if unavailable)
- 1/2 onion, sliced
- 1 red bell pepper, sliced
- 1/4 cup soy sauce
- 1 tablespoon fish sauce
- 1 tablespoon sugar
- 1/4 cup fresh basil leaves
- 1 teaspoon lime juice
- Cooked rice, for serving

Instructions:

1. **Cook the Chicken**:
   Heat vegetable oil in a large skillet over medium-high heat. Add the garlic and chilies and cook for 1-2 minutes until fragrant. Add the chicken slices and cook until browned and cooked through, about 6-7 minutes.
2. **Add Vegetables**:
   Add the onion and red bell pepper to the skillet and cook for another 2-3 minutes, until the vegetables soften.
3. **Make the Sauce**:
   Stir in the soy sauce, fish sauce, and sugar. Cook for 1-2 minutes, allowing the sauce to reduce slightly.
4. **Finish with Basil and Lime**:
   Add the fresh basil leaves and lime juice. Toss everything together until the basil wilts.
5. **Serve**:
   Serve the Thai basil chicken over a bed of rice for a satisfying meal.

Coconut Milk and Chickpea Soup

Ingredients:

- 1 tablespoon olive oil
- 1 onion, chopped
- 2 cloves garlic, minced
- 1 can (15 oz) chickpeas, drained and rinsed
- 1 can (13.5 oz) coconut milk
- 2 cups vegetable broth
- 1 teaspoon ground cumin
- 1 teaspoon curry powder
- 1/2 teaspoon turmeric
- Salt and pepper, to taste
- Fresh cilantro, for garnish
- Lime wedges, for serving

Instructions:

1. **Sauté the Aromatics**:
   In a large pot, heat olive oil over medium heat. Add the chopped onion and garlic and cook for 3-4 minutes until softened.
2. **Add the Spices**:
   Stir in cumin, curry powder, and turmeric, and cook for 1 minute until fragrant.
3. **Make the Soup**:
   Add chickpeas, coconut milk, and vegetable broth to the pot. Bring to a simmer and cook for 10-15 minutes, allowing the flavors to meld. Season with salt and pepper to taste.
4. **Blend (Optional)**:
   For a smoother soup, use an immersion blender to blend the soup slightly or completely, depending on your preference.
5. **Serve**:
   Serve the soup hot, garnished with fresh cilantro and lime wedges.

Grilled Tofu Skewers

Ingredients:

- 1 block firm tofu, pressed and cut into cubes
- 1 tablespoon olive oil
- 2 tablespoons soy sauce or tamari
- 1 tablespoon maple syrup or agave nectar
- 1 teaspoon garlic powder
- 1 teaspoon smoked paprika
- Salt and pepper, to taste
- 1 tablespoon sesame oil (optional)
- 1 tablespoon sesame seeds (optional)
- Fresh cilantro or parsley for garnish

Instructions:

1. **Prepare the Marinade**:
   In a bowl, whisk together olive oil, soy sauce, maple syrup, garlic powder, smoked paprika, salt, and pepper.
2. **Marinate the Tofu**:
   Place the tofu cubes in a shallow dish and pour the marinade over them. Toss to coat and let the tofu marinate for at least 30 minutes.
3. **Grill the Tofu**:
   Preheat your grill or grill pan to medium heat. Thread the tofu cubes onto skewers (if using wooden skewers, soak them in water for 10 minutes before use). Grill the tofu skewers for 4-5 minutes on each side until lightly charred.
4. **Serve**:
   Drizzle with sesame oil (optional) and sprinkle with sesame seeds. Garnish with fresh cilantro or parsley. Serve warm with your favorite side dish.

Cabbage Stir-Fry with Peanut Sauce

Ingredients:

- 1/2 head of cabbage, thinly sliced
- 1 tablespoon olive oil
- 1 carrot, julienned
- 1 bell pepper, sliced
- 1/2 onion, sliced
- 2 cloves garlic, minced
- 1 tablespoon fresh ginger, grated
- 1 tablespoon soy sauce or tamari
- 1 tablespoon rice vinegar
- 1 tablespoon peanut butter
- 1 teaspoon maple syrup
- 1/4 cup water
- 1 teaspoon sesame oil
- 1 tablespoon sesame seeds (optional)
- Fresh cilantro, for garnish

Instructions:

1. **Make the Peanut Sauce:**
   In a small bowl, whisk together soy sauce, rice vinegar, peanut butter, maple syrup, and water until smooth. Set aside.
2. **Stir-Fry the Vegetables:**
   Heat olive oil in a large skillet or wok over medium heat. Add the onion, carrot, bell pepper, and garlic, and sauté for 5-7 minutes until the vegetables are tender.
3. **Add the Cabbage:**
   Add the sliced cabbage and cook for an additional 3-4 minutes until the cabbage softens but still has a bit of crunch.
4. **Add the Peanut Sauce:**
   Pour the peanut sauce over the stir-fried vegetables and toss to coat evenly. Drizzle with sesame oil and stir in sesame seeds if desired.
5. **Serve:**
   Serve warm, garnished with fresh cilantro.

Spaghetti with Roasted Garlic and Spinach

Ingredients:

- 8 oz spaghetti (gluten-free, if preferred)
- 1 tablespoon olive oil
- 10 cloves garlic, peeled
- 4 cups fresh spinach
- 1 tablespoon lemon juice
- Salt and pepper, to taste
- Grated Parmesan cheese, for serving (optional)

Instructions:

1. **Roast the Garlic**:
   Preheat your oven to 400°F (200°C). Place the garlic cloves on a piece of aluminum foil, drizzle with olive oil, and wrap tightly. Roast in the oven for 20-25 minutes, until the garlic is soft and golden.
2. **Cook the Spaghetti**:
   While the garlic is roasting, cook the spaghetti according to package instructions. Drain and set aside.
3. **Sauté the Spinach**:
   In a large skillet, heat a little olive oil over medium heat. Add the spinach and sauté until wilted, about 2-3 minutes.
4. **Mash the Garlic**:
   Once the garlic is roasted, mash the cloves with a fork and add to the skillet with the spinach. Stir to combine and cook for another 2 minutes.
5. **Combine**:
   Add the cooked spaghetti to the skillet and toss to coat in the roasted garlic and spinach mixture. Drizzle with lemon juice and season with salt and pepper.
6. **Serve**:
   Serve warm with grated Parmesan cheese (optional).

Vegan Sweet Potato Shepherd's Pie

Ingredients:

- 3 medium sweet potatoes, peeled and cubed
- 1 tablespoon olive oil
- 1 onion, chopped
- 2 cloves garlic, minced
- 1 cup mushrooms, chopped
- 1 cup peas (frozen or fresh)
- 1 cup carrots, diced
- 1 can (15 oz) lentils, drained and rinsed
- 1 cup vegetable broth
- 1 teaspoon dried thyme
- Salt and pepper, to taste
- 1 tablespoon nutritional yeast (optional)

Instructions:

1. **Cook the Sweet Potatoes**:
   Boil the sweet potatoes in a large pot of salted water for 10-12 minutes, until tender. Drain and mash with olive oil, salt, and pepper. Set aside.
2. **Sauté the Vegetables**:
   In a large skillet, heat olive oil over medium heat. Add the onion, garlic, mushrooms, carrots, and peas. Sauté for 5-7 minutes until the vegetables are tender.
3. **Make the Filling**:
   Add the lentils, vegetable broth, and dried thyme to the skillet. Stir to combine and simmer for 5-7 minutes until heated through. Season with salt and pepper.
4. **Assemble the Shepherd's Pie**:
   Preheat your oven to 375°F (190°C). Transfer the vegetable and lentil mixture into a baking dish. Spread the mashed sweet potatoes on top, smoothing the surface.
5. **Bake**:
   Bake for 20 minutes, until the top is slightly golden. Optionally, sprinkle with nutritional yeast for a cheesy flavor.
6. **Serve**:
   Serve warm as a comforting, hearty meal.

BBQ Grilled Chicken with Roasted Sweet Potatoes

Ingredients:

- 4 boneless, skinless chicken breasts
- 1/2 cup BBQ sauce (store-bought or homemade)
- 2 large sweet potatoes, cubed
- 1 tablespoon olive oil
- 1 teaspoon smoked paprika
- Salt and pepper, to taste
- Fresh parsley, for garnish

Instructions:

1. **Prepare the Chicken**:
   Brush the chicken breasts with BBQ sauce and let them marinate for at least 20 minutes.
2. **Roast the Sweet Potatoes**:
   Preheat your oven to 400°F (200°C). Toss the cubed sweet potatoes with olive oil, smoked paprika, salt, and pepper. Spread them out on a baking sheet and roast for 25-30 minutes, until tender.
3. **Grill the Chicken**:
   Preheat the grill to medium-high heat. Grill the chicken for 5-7 minutes per side, until fully cooked and the internal temperature reaches 165°F (74°C).
4. **Serve**:
   Serve the BBQ chicken with roasted sweet potatoes, garnished with fresh parsley.

Mango and Black Bean Salad

Ingredients:

- 1 ripe mango, diced
- 1 can (15 oz) black beans, drained and rinsed
- 1 red bell pepper, diced
- 1/4 red onion, finely chopped
- 1/4 cup cilantro, chopped
- 1 tablespoon lime juice
- Salt and pepper, to taste

Instructions:

1. **Combine the Ingredients:**
   In a large bowl, combine the mango, black beans, bell pepper, onion, and cilantro.
2. **Dress the Salad:**
   Drizzle with lime juice and season with salt and pepper. Toss gently to combine.
3. **Serve:**
   Serve immediately as a refreshing side dish or light meal.

www.ingramcontent.com/pod-product-compliance
Lightning Source LLC
LaVergne TN
LVHW081335060526
838201LV00055B/2652